GRACE-FILLED GRATITUDE:
A 40-DAY JOY JOURNAL

WITH INSPIRATIONAL SCRIPTURES

D0066907

THIS JOURNAL BELONGS TO:

_____

ISBN: 978-0-578-82370-6

FREE GIFT!

I'd love to share a free copy of my **"Ten Commandments of Joy"** with you!

This is a fun reminder of how to claim your joy in ALL circumstances.

It also has an accompanying video!

Just go to: http://susansparks.com/ten-commandments-opt-in/ and click **FREE GIFT!**

ALSO BY SUSAN SPARKS

Laugh Your Way to Grace:
Reclaiming the Spiritual Power of Humor

Preaching Punchlines: The Ten Commandments of Comedy

Miracle on 31ˢᵗ Street:
Christmas Cheer Every Day of the Year – Grinch to Gratitude in 26
Days!

Love, a Tiara, and a Cupcake: Three Secrets to Finding Happy
(coming February 14, 2021 on Amazon!)

INTRODUCTION

WELCOME!

I'm so glad that you decided to join me on this 40-day journey to joy and grace-filled gratitude!

These days, it's hard to remember to be thankful. Our gratitude is held at bay by things like fear, anxiety, abrupt life changes, job loss, aging parents, financial stress, family tensions, and health worries. Truly, the world tries to beat gratitude right out of us. But like the tiny spark of hope in our hearts that drives it . . .

It's. Still. There.

Join me, Rev. Susan Sparks, a trial lawyer turned stand-up comedian and Baptist minister, as we reveal, remember, and rediscover the healing power of joy and grace-filled gratitude in our daily lives.

I call it "grace-filled" thanks to my paternal grandmother, Grace Foster Sparks, who lived in Gaffney, South Carolina. In fact, I'm named after her: Susan Grace Sparks. While great theologians such as Martin Luther and St. Augustine have attempted to describe grace in powerful ways, I believe the home of Grace Foster Sparks provides the best image of all.

A tiny, rather squishy woman, Ganny, as we called her, gave hugs that felt like being pressed into a fluffy feather pillow. And . . . she always had a special treat ready to share! My favorite was the cherry pie from the A&P grocery store. Ganny knew that I didn't like pie crust, so she would peel away the shell and feed me spoonfuls of the cherry insides. (And no, I was not spoiled. Okay, maybe a little.)

To me, grace is the same thing as Ganny's house: a place of grounding and belonging where you feel special, like you are wrapped in an inordinately long, squishy hug, eating the filling out of a pie. (To read more about this take on grace, check out my blog post "A Place Called Grace!" http://susansparks.com/blog/a-place-called-grace/)

We all need to find that place. But it's hard. Every day we are bombarded by corrosive voices from the outside world that eat away at our sense of self. We are assaulted by negative words that tear us down, make us slump over in shame, cause us to feel less than the beloved children of God that we are. We need to find that place called grace.

Take heart, my friends. It's still there. Like a tiny breeze over an ember, it starts to glow when we see the sun rise, watch the change of seasons, hear the laughter of a little child, or read one of the beautiful scriptures in this journal. It brightens when we remember that we are not alone, and that we are part of something bigger. It shines full force when we connect back to our source, remembering that we are loved, that we are worthy, and that we matter.

When grace shines out, our hearts begin to open, and our spirits start to rise. The bounty of blessings around us becomes high-definition crystal clear. It's then—when we start to consistently see our blessings and articulate our gratitude—that grace blossoms into its fullest state: "grace-filled gratitude."

The ultimate question is how to introduce this grace-filled gratitude into our daily grind.

We must start by cutting through the noise, stress, and negativity so that we might begin to listen to what God and the scriptures have to teach us. It's about deep soul work. It's about a housecleaning of the heart.

And that's where this journal comes in! For the next forty days, we will be concentrating on shifting our perspective and letting go of all the things that block us from our God-given gifts of gratitude and joy. In short, we will be focusing on getting out of our own way. As one of my favorite authors, Anne Lamott, once said, "God can't clean the house of you with you in it."

I chose forty days for the length of the journal, as forty is a number of great significance in the Bible. Moses was on Mount Sinai for forty days receiving the Ten Commandments. The rains of the great flood lasted forty days before creation was given a second chance. And Jesus fasted for forty days and nights to prepare for his ministry. Forty is a sacred number relating to change and renewal, just as these forty days will be a time of sacred transformation for you.

Each day of this journal starts with an inspirational scripture relating to themes like gratitude, joy, fear, worry, letting go, and faith. These are some of my favorite scriptures gathered over my twenty years as a pastor. They draw from all parts of the Bible – each one offering a deep and profound well of comfort and insight.

I have also crafted a specific set of journaling prompts for these scriptures. They are based on a tradition called Lectio Divina or "divine reading." While there are many versions of this practice, here is my six-step suggestion:

1. Start by finding a quiet place. Take a few deep breaths, then say a short prayer inviting God's presence. I use words based on Psalm 46: "Be still and know that the power of God is near." This is holy space—sacred time.

2. Turn to the day's scripture. Read the scripture several times out loud, paying attention to the word or phrase that strikes you from the reading. You may want to underline or circle it. How is God speaking to you in this word or phrase?

3. Read the scripture out loud a second time. Where in your life do you need this word, this lesson?

4. Take a moment of silence to rest in God's presence. Imagine how your life would be different if you put the lesson into action.

5. As a final part of the ritual, name three things for which you are grateful. This is an important daily pattern to nurture. It ensures that gratitude will become habit—a habit which can completely change how you see the world.

6. Finish your sacred time by letting go with the Serenity Prayer: "God, grant me the serenity to accept the things I cannot change, the courage to change the things I can, and the wisdom to know the

difference."

That will be your rhythm for the next forty days.

At the end of this journal, I have included a short exercise that invites you to focus on what you've learned, contemplate the significance, then, craft a commitment plan to build a personal foundation for experiencing "grace-filled gratitude" every day of your life.

There is power in committing yourself to consistent daily introspection, prayer, and spiritual development. How we spend our time and choose our priorities drives our life's trajectory. To paraphrase the author and philosopher Ralph Waldo Emerson, what we worship we become. May we always place grace-filled gratitude at the forefront.

I congratulate you on this commitment and wish you many blessings on this sacred journey.

Let's get started! xo Susan

Day 1

Opening Prayer: "Be still and know that the power of God is near."

Daily Scripture: *"Do not fear, for I am with you; do not anxiously look about you, for I am your God. I will strengthen you, surely, I will help you, surely, I will uphold you with My righteous right hand." (Isaiah 41:10)*

Which part of this scripture most resonates with you?

_____

_____

_____

_____

_____

_____

[THERE ARE PLENTY OF EXTRA PAGES WITH SPACE TO WRITE IN THE BACK!]

Where in your life do you need these words?

_____

_____

_____

_____

_____

_____

How would your life change if you applied this lesson?

_____

_____

_____

_____

_____

_____

_____

Name three things for which you are grateful today:

1)_____

_____

2)_____

_____

3)_____

_____

The Serenity Prayer:

God, grant me the serenity to accept the things I cannot change,
the courage to change the things I can, and the wisdom to know the
difference.

Day 2

Opening Prayer: "Be still and know that the power of God is near."

Daily Scripture: *"This is the day that the Lord has made; let us rejoice and be glad in it." (Psalm 118:24)*

Which part of this scripture most resonates with you?

_____

_____

_____

_____

_____

_____

Where in your life do you need these words?

_____

_____

_____

_____

_____

_____

How would your life change if you applied this lesson?

_____

_____

_____

_____

_____

_____

_____

Name three things for which you are grateful today:

1)_____

_____

2)_____

_____

3)_____

_____

The Serenity Prayer:
God, grant me the serenity to accept the things I cannot change,
the courage to change the things I can, and the wisdom to know the
difference.

Day 3

Opening Prayer: "Be still and know that the power of God is near."

Daily Scripture: *"Know this, my beloved brothers: let every person be quick to hear, slow to speak, slow to anger." (James 1:19)*

Which part of this scripture most resonates with you?

_____

_____

_____

_____

_____

_____

_____

Where in your life do you need these words?

_____

_____

_____

_____

_____

_____

_____

How would your life change if you applied this lesson?

_____

_____

_____

_____

_____

_____

_____

Name three things for which you are grateful today:

1)_____

_____

2)_____

_____

3)_____

_____

The Serenity Prayer:
God, grant me the serenity to accept the things I cannot change,
the courage to change the things I can, and the wisdom to know the
difference.

Day 4

Opening Prayer: "Be still and know that the power of God is near."

Daily Scripture: *"Do not let the sun go down on your anger."*
(Ephesians 4:26)

Which part of this scripture most resonates with you?

_____

_____

_____

_____

_____

_____

_____

Where in your life do you need these words?

_____

_____

_____

_____

_____

_____

_____

How would your life change if you applied this lesson?

_____

_____

_____

_____

_____

_____

_____

Name three things for which you are grateful today:

1)_____

_____

2)_____

_____

3)_____

_____

The Serenity Prayer:

God, grant me the serenity to accept the things I cannot change,
the courage to change the things I can, and the wisdom to know the
difference.

Day 5

Opening Prayer: "Be still and know that the power of God is near."

Daily Scripture: *"Set a guard over my mouth, Lord; keep watch over the door of my lips." (Psalm 141:3)*

Which part of this scripture most resonates with you?

_____

_____

_____

_____

_____

_____

Where in your life do you need these words?

_____

_____

_____

_____

_____

_____

_____

How would your life change if you applied this lesson?

_____

_____

_____

_____

_____

_____

_____

Name three things for which you are grateful today:

1)_____

_____

2)_____

_____

3)_____

_____

The Serenity Prayer:
God, grant me the serenity to accept the things I cannot change,
the courage to change the things I can, and the wisdom to know the
difference.

Day 6

Opening Prayer: "Be still and know that the power of God is near."

Daily Scripture: *"Remember not the former things, nor consider the things of old. Behold, I am doing a new thing; now it springs forth, do you not perceive it? I will make a way in the wilderness and rivers in the desert." (Isaiah 43:18-19)*

Which part of this scripture most resonates with you?

_____

_____

_____

_____

_____

_____

_____

Where in your life do you need these words?

_____

_____

_____

_____

_____

_____

_____

How would your life change if you applied this lesson?

_____

_____

_____

_____

_____

_____

_____

Name three things for which you are grateful today:

1)_____

_____

2)_____

_____

3)_____

_____

The Serenity Prayer:
God, grant me the serenity to accept the things I cannot change,
the courage to change the things I can, and the wisdom to know the
difference.

Day 7

Opening Prayer: "Be still and know that the power of God is near."

Daily Scripture: *"Cast all your anxieties on him, because he cares for you." (1 Peter 5:7)*

Which part of this scripture most resonates with you?

_____

_____

_____

_____

_____

_____

_____

Where in your life do you need these words?

_____

_____

_____

_____

_____

_____

_____

How would your life change if you applied this lesson?

_____

_____

_____

_____

_____

_____

_____

Name three things for which you are grateful today:

1)_____

_____

2)_____

_____

3)_____

_____

The Serenity Prayer:

God, grant me the serenity to accept the things I cannot change,
the courage to change the things I can, and the wisdom to know the
difference.

Day 8

Opening Prayer: "Be still and know that the power of God is near."

Daily Scripture: *"Let all bitterness and wrath and anger and clamor and slander be put away from you, along with all malice. Be kind to one another, tenderhearted, forgiving one another, as God in Christ forgave you." (Ephesians 4:31-32)*

Which part of this scripture most resonates with you?

_____

_____

_____

_____

_____

_____

_____

Where in your life do you need these words?

_____

_____

_____

_____

_____

_____

_____

How would your life change if you applied this lesson?

_____

_____

_____

_____

_____

_____

_____

Name three things for which you are grateful today:

1)_____

_____

2)_____

_____

3)_____

_____

The Serenity Prayer:
God, grant me the serenity to accept the things I cannot change,
the courage to change the things I can, and the wisdom to know the
difference.

Day 9

Opening Prayer: "Be still and know that the power of God is near."

Daily Scripture: *"Let your eyes look directly forward, and your gaze be straight before you. Ponder the path of your feet; then all your ways will be sure. Do not swerve to the right or to the left; turn your foot away from evil." (Proverbs 4:25-27)*

Which part of this scripture most resonates with you?

_____

_____

_____

_____

_____

_____

_____

Where in your life do you need these words?

_____

_____

_____

_____

_____

_____

_____

How would your life change if you applied this lesson?

_____

_____

_____

_____

_____

_____

_____

Name three things for which you are grateful today:

1)_____

_____

2)_____

_____

3)_____

_____

The Serenity Prayer:
God, grant me the serenity to accept the things I cannot change,
the courage to change the things I can, and the wisdom to know the
difference.

Day 10

Opening Prayer: "Be still and know that the power of God is near."

Daily Scripture: *"And you will know the truth, and the truth will set you free." (John 8:32)*

Which part of this scripture most resonates with you?

_____

_____

_____

_____

_____

_____

_____

Where in your life do you need these words?

_____

_____

_____

_____

_____

_____

_____

How would your life change if you applied this lesson?

_____

_____

_____

_____

_____

_____

_____

Name three things for which you are grateful today:

1)_____

_____

2)_____

_____

3)_____

_____

The Serenity Prayer:
God, grant me the serenity to accept the things I cannot change, the courage to change the things I can, and the wisdom to know the difference.

Day 11

Opening Prayer: "Be still and know that the power of God is near."

Daily Scripture*: "A time to seek, and a time to lose; a time to keep, and a time to cast away." (Ecclesiastes 3:6)*

Which part of this scripture most resonates with you?

_____

_____

_____

_____

_____

_____

_____

Where in your life do you need these words?

_____

_____

_____

_____

_____

_____

_____

How would your life change if you applied this lesson?

_____

_____

_____

_____

_____

_____

_____

Name three things for which you are grateful today:

1)_____

_____

2)_____

_____

3)_____

_____

The Serenity Prayer:
God, grant me the serenity to accept the things I cannot change,
the courage to change the things I can, and the wisdom to know the
difference.

Day 12

Opening Prayer: "Be still and know that the power of God is near."

Daily Scripture: *"Come to me, all who labor and are heavy laden, and I will give you rest. Take my yoke upon you, and learn from me, for I am gentle and lowly in heart, and you will find rest for your souls. For my yoke is easy, and my burden is light."*
(Matthew 11:28-30)

Which part of this scripture most resonates with you?

_____

_____

_____

_____

_____

_____

_____

Where in your life do you need these words?

_____

_____

_____

_____

_____

_____

How would your life change if you applied this lesson?

_____

_____

_____

_____

_____

_____

_____

Name three things for which you are grateful today:

1)_____

_____

2)_____

_____

3)_____

_____

The Serenity Prayer:

God, grant me the serenity to accept the things I cannot change,
the courage to change the things I can, and the wisdom to know the
difference.

Day 13

Opening Prayer: "Be still and know that the power of God is near."

Daily Scripture: *"Judge not, and you will not be judged; condemn not, and you will not be condemned; forgive, and you will be forgiven." (Luke 6:37)*

Which part of this scripture most resonates with you?

_____

_____

_____

_____

_____

_____

_____

Where in your life do you need these words?

_____

_____

_____

_____

_____

_____

_____

How would your life change if you applied this lesson?

_____

_____

_____

_____

_____

_____

_____

Name three things for which you are grateful today:

1)_____

_____

2)_____

_____

3)_____

_____

The Serenity Prayer:

God, grant me the serenity to accept the things I cannot change, the courage to change the things I can, and the wisdom to know the difference.

Day 14

Opening Prayer: "Be still and know that the power of God is near."

Daily Scripture: *"And which of you by being anxious can add a single hour to his span of life?" (Matthew 6:27)*

Which part of this scripture most resonates with you?

_____

_____

_____

_____

_____

_____

_____

Where in your life do you need these words?

_____

_____

_____

_____

_____

_____

_____

How would your life change if you applied this lesson?

_____

_____

_____

_____

_____

_____

_____

Name three things for which you are grateful today:

1)_____

_____

2)_____

_____

3)_____

_____

The Serenity Prayer:
God, grant me the serenity to accept the things I cannot change, the courage to change the things I can, and the wisdom to know the difference.

Day 15

Opening Prayer: "Be still and know that the power of God is near."

Daily Scripture: *"Have I not commanded you? Be strong and courageous. Do not be frightened, and do not be dismayed, for the Lord your God is with you wherever you go." (Joshua 1:9)*

Which part of this scripture most resonates with you?

_____

_____

_____

_____

_____

_____

_____

Where in your life do you need these words?

_____

_____

_____

_____

_____

_____

_____

How would your life change if you applied this lesson?

_____

_____

_____

_____

_____

_____

_____

Name three things for which you are grateful today:

1)_____

_____

2)_____

_____

3)_____

_____

The Serenity Prayer:

God, grant me the serenity to accept the things I cannot change, the courage to change the things I can, and the wisdom to know the difference.

Day 16

Opening Prayer: "Be still and know that the power of God is near."

Daily Scripture: *"Give thanks in all circumstances, for this is the will of God in Christ Jesus for you." (1 Thessalonians 5:18)*

Which part of this scripture most resonates with you?

_____

_____

_____

_____

_____

_____

_____

Where in your life do you need these words?

_____

_____

_____

_____

_____

_____

_____

How would your life change if you applied this lesson?

_____

_____

_____

_____

_____

_____

_____

Name three things for which you are grateful today:

1)_____

_____

2)_____

_____

3)_____

_____

The Serenity Prayer:

God, grant me the serenity to accept the things I cannot change,
the courage to change the things I can, and the wisdom to know the
difference.

Day 17

Opening Prayer: "Be still and know that the power of God is near."

Daily Scripture: *"But I say to you, love your enemies and pray for those who persecute you." (Matthew 5:44)*

Which part of this scripture most resonates with you?

_____

_____

_____

_____

_____

_____

_____

Where in your life do you need these words?

_____

_____

_____

_____

_____

_____

_____

How would your life change if you applied this lesson?

_____

_____

_____

_____

_____

_____

_____

Name three things for which you are grateful today:

1)_____

_____

2)_____

_____

3)_____

_____

The Serenity Prayer:

God, grant me the serenity to accept the things I cannot change,
the courage to change the things I can, and the wisdom to know the
difference.

Day 18

Opening Prayer: "Be still and know that the power of God is near."

Daily Scripture: *"Every good gift and every perfect gift is from above, coming down from the Father of lights with whom there is no variation or shadow due to change." (James 1:17)*

Which part of this scripture most resonates with you?

_____

_____

_____

_____

_____

_____

_____

Where in your life do you need these words?

_____

_____

_____

_____

_____

_____

_____

How would your life change if you applied this lesson?

_____

_____

_____

_____

_____

_____

_____

Name three things for which you are grateful today:

1)_____

_____

2)_____

_____

3)_____

_____

The Serenity Prayer:

God, grant me the serenity to accept the things I cannot change,
the courage to change the things I can, and the wisdom to know the
difference.

Day 19

Opening Prayer: "Be still and know that the power of God is near."

Daily Scripture: *"I lift up mine eyes to the hills, from whence com-
eth my help. My help comes from the Lord who made heaven and
earth. He will not let your foot be moved; he who keeps you will not
sleep." (Psalm 121:1-3)*

Which part of this scripture most resonates with you?

_____

_____

_____

_____

_____

_____

_____

Where in your life do you need these words?

_____

_____

_____

_____

_____

_____

_____

How would your life change if you applied this lesson?

_____

_____

_____

_____

_____

_____

_____

Name three things for which you are grateful today:

1)_____

_____

2)_____

_____

3)_____

_____

The Serenity Prayer:
God, grant me the serenity to accept the things I cannot change,
the courage to change the things I can, and the wisdom to know the
difference.

Day 20

Opening Prayer: "Be still and know that the power of God is near."

Daily Scripture: *"Do not forget to show hospitality to strangers, for by so doing some people have shown hospitality to angels without knowing it." (Hebrews 13:2)*

Which part of this scripture most resonates with you?

_____

_____

_____

_____

_____

_____

_____

Where in your life do you need these words?

_____

_____

_____

_____

_____

_____

_____

How would your life change if you applied this lesson?

_____

_____

_____

_____

_____

_____

_____

Name three things for which you are grateful today:

1)_____

_____

2)_____

_____

3)_____

_____

The Serenity Prayer:
God, grant me the serenity to accept the things I cannot change,
the courage to change the things I can, and the wisdom to know the
difference.

Day 21

Opening Prayer: "Be still and know that the power of God is near."

Daily Scripture: *"You will be enriched in every way so that you can be generous on every occasion, and through us your generosity will result in thanksgiving to God. This service that you perform is not only supplying the needs of the Lord's people, but is also overflowing in many expressions of thanks to God." (2 Corinthians 9:11-12)*

Which part of this scripture most resonates with you?

_____

_____

_____

_____

_____

_____

_____

Where in your life do you need these words?

_____

_____

_____

_____

_____

_____

_____

How would your life change if you applied this lesson?

_____

_____

_____

_____

_____

_____

_____

Name three things for which you are grateful today:

1)_____

_____

2)_____

_____

3)_____

_____

The Serenity Prayer:
God, grant me the serenity to accept the things I cannot change,
the courage to change the things I can, and the wisdom to know the
difference.

Day 22

Opening Prayer: "Be still and know that the power of God is near."

Daily Scripture: *"He alone is my rock and my salvation. He is my fortress where I shall not be shaken."* (Psalm 62:6)

Which part of this scripture most resonates with you?

_____

_____

_____

_____

_____

_____

_____

Where in your life do you need these words?

_____

_____

_____

_____

_____

_____

_____

How would your life change if you applied this lesson?

_____

_____

_____

_____

_____

_____

_____

Name three things for which you are grateful today:

1)_____

_____

2)_____

_____

3)_____

_____

The Serenity Prayer:
God, grant me the serenity to accept the things I cannot change,
the courage to change the things I can, and the wisdom to know the
difference.

51

Day 23

Opening Prayer: "Be still and know that the power of God is near."

Daily Scripture: *"Do not be anxious about anything, but in everything, by prayer and petition, with thanksgiving, present your requests to God. And the peace of God, which transcends all understanding, will guard your hearts and your minds in Christ Jesus." (Philippians 4:6-7)*

Which part of this scripture most resonates with you?

_____

_____

_____

_____

_____

_____

Where in your life do you need these words?

_____

_____

_____

_____

_____

_____

How would your life change if you applied this lesson?

_____

_____

_____

_____

_____

_____

_____

Name three things for which you are grateful today:

1)_____

_____

2)_____

_____

3)_____

_____

The Serenity Prayer:
God, grant me the serenity to accept the things I cannot change,
the courage to change the things I can, and the wisdom to know the
difference.

Day 24

Opening Prayer: "Be still and know that the power of God is near."

Daily Scripture: *"... Thus says the LORD, the God of David your father: I have heard your prayer, I have seen your tears; surely, I will heal you." (2 Kings 20:5)*

Which part of this scripture most resonates with you?

_____

_____

_____

_____

_____

_____

_____

Where in your life do you need these words?

_____

_____

_____

_____

_____

_____

_____

How would your life change if you applied this lesson?

_____

_____

_____

_____

_____

_____

_____

Name three things for which you are grateful today:

1)_____

_____

2)_____

_____

3)_____

_____

The Serenity Prayer:
God, grant me the serenity to accept the things I cannot change,
the courage to change the things I can, and the wisdom to know the
difference.

Day 25

Opening Prayer: "Be still and know that the power of God is near."

Daily Scripture: *"Cast your burden on the Lord, and He will sustain you; He will never allow the righteous to be moved." (Psalm 55:22)*

Which part of this scripture most resonates with you?

_____

_____

_____

_____

_____

_____

_____

Where in your life do you need these words?

_____

_____

_____

_____

_____

_____

_____

How would your life change if you applied this lesson?

_____

_____

_____

_____

_____

_____

_____

Name three things for which you are grateful today:

1)_____

_____

2)_____

_____

3)_____

_____

The Serenity Prayer:
God, grant me the serenity to accept the things I cannot change,
the courage to change the things I can, and the wisdom to know the
difference.

Day 26

Opening Prayer: "Be still and know that the power of God is near."

Daily Scripture: *"In every way and everywhere we accept this with all gratitude." (Acts 24:3)*

Which part of this scripture most resonates with you?

_____

_____

_____

_____

_____

_____

_____

Where in your life do you need these words?

_____

_____

_____

_____

_____

_____

_____

How would your life change if you applied this lesson?

_____

_____

_____

_____

_____

_____

_____

Name three things for which you are grateful today:

1)_____

_____

2)_____

_____

3)_____

_____

The Serenity Prayer:
God, grant me the serenity to accept the things I cannot change,
the courage to change the things I can, and the wisdom to know the
difference.

Day 27

Opening Prayer: "Be still and know that the power of God is near."

Daily Scripture: *"Whatever you ask for in Prayer with faith, you will receive." (Matthew 21:22)*

Which part of this scripture most resonates with you?

_____

_____

_____

_____

_____

_____

_____

_____

Where in your life do you need these words?

_____

_____

_____

_____

_____

_____

_____

How would your life change if you applied this lesson?

_____

_____

_____

_____

_____

_____

_____

Name three things for which you are grateful today:

1)_____

_____

2)_____

_____

3)_____

_____

The Serenity Prayer:
God, grant me the serenity to accept the things I cannot change,
the courage to change the things I can, and the wisdom to know the
difference.

Day 28

Opening Prayer: "Be still and know that the power of God is near."

Daily Scripture: *"Be merciful to me, O God, be merciful to me, for in you my soul takes refuge; in the shadow of your wings I will take refuge, until the destroying storms pass by." (Psalm 57:1)*

Which part of this scripture most resonates with you?

_____

_____

_____

_____

_____

_____

_____

Where in your life do you need these words?

_____

_____

_____

_____

_____

_____

_____

How would your life change if you applied this lesson?

_____

_____

_____

_____

_____

_____

_____

Name three things for which you are grateful today:

1)_____

_____

2)_____

_____

3)_____

_____

The Serenity Prayer:
God, grant me the serenity to accept the things I cannot change,
the courage to change the things I can, and the wisdom to know the
difference.

Day 29

Opening Prayer: "Be still and know that the power of God is near."

Daily Scripture: *"I do not cease to give thanks for you, remembering you in my prayers." (Ephesians 1:16)*

Which part of this scripture most resonates with you?

_____

_____

_____

_____

_____

_____

_____

Where in your life do you need these words?

_____

_____

_____

_____

_____

_____

_____

How would your life change if you applied this lesson?

_____

_____

_____

_____

_____

_____

_____

Name three things for which you are grateful today:

1)_____

_____

2)_____

_____

3)_____

_____

The Serenity Prayer:
God, grant me the serenity to accept the things I cannot change,
the courage to change the things I can, and the wisdom to know the
difference.

Day 30

Opening Prayer: "Be still and know that the power of God is near."

Daily Scripture: *"Make a joyful noise to the Lord, all the earth! Serve the Lord with gladness! Come into his presence with singing! Know that the Lord, he is God! It is he who made us, and we are his; we are his people, and the sheep of his pasture. Enter his gates with thanksgiving, and his courts with praise! Give thanks to him; bless his name! For the Lord is good; his steadfast love endures forever, and his faithfulness to all generations." (Psalm 100:1-5)*

Which part of this scripture most resonates with you?

_____

_____

_____

_____

_____

_____

Where in your life do you need these words?

_____

_____

_____

_____

_____

_____

How would your life change if you applied this lesson?

_____

_____

_____

_____

_____

_____

_____

Name three things for which you are grateful today:

1)_____

_____

2)_____

_____

3)_____

_____

The Serenity Prayer:
God, grant me the serenity to accept the things I cannot change,
the courage to change the things I can, and the wisdom to know the
difference.

Day 31

Opening Prayer: "Be still and know that the power of God is near."

Daily Scripture: *"Stand firm then, with the belt of truth buckled around your waist, with the breastplate of righteousness in place, and with your feet fitted with the readiness that comes from the gospel of peace." (Ephesians 6:14-16)*

Which part of this scripture most resonates with you?

_____

_____

_____

_____

_____

_____

_____

Where in your life do you need these words?

_____

_____

_____

_____

_____

_____

_____

How would your life change if you applied this lesson?

_____

_____

_____

_____

_____

_____

_____

Name three things for which you are grateful today:

1)_____

_____

2)_____

_____

3)_____

_____

The Serenity Prayer:
God, grant me the serenity to accept the things I cannot change,
the courage to change the things I can, and the wisdom to know the
diffcrence.

Day 32

Opening Prayer: "Be still and know that the power of God is near."

Daily Scripture: *"Then your light shall break forth like the morning, your healing shall spring forth speedily, and your righteousness shall go before you; The glory of the LORD shall be your rear guard."*
(Isaiah 58:8)

Which part of this scripture most resonates with you?

_____

_____

_____

_____

_____

_____

_____

Where in your life do you need these words?

_____

_____

_____

_____

_____

_____

_____

How would your life change if you applied this lesson?

_____

_____

_____

_____

_____

_____

_____

Name three things for which you are grateful today:

1)_____

_____

2)_____

_____

3)_____

_____

The Serenity Prayer:
God, grant me the serenity to accept the things I cannot change,
the courage to change the things I can, and the wisdom to know the
difference.

Day 33

Opening Prayer: "Be still and know that the power of God is near."

Daily Scripture: *"Truly, I say unto you, whatsoever you shall bind on earth shall be bound in heaven: and whatsoever you shall loose on earth shall be loosed in heaven." (Matthew 18:18)*

Which part of this scripture most resonates with you?

_____

_____

_____

_____

_____

_____

_____

Where in your life do you need these words?

_____

_____

_____

_____

_____

_____

_____

How would your life change if you applied this lesson?

_____

_____

_____

_____

_____

_____

_____

Name three things for which you are grateful today:

1)_____

_____

2)_____

_____

3)_____

_____

The Serenity Prayer:
God, grant me the serenity to accept the things I cannot change,
the courage to change the things I can, and the wisdom to know the
difference.

Day 34

Opening Prayer: "Be still and know that the power of God is near."

Daily Scripture: *"For he will command his angels concerning you to guard you in all your ways. On their hands they will bear you up, so that you will not dash your foot against a stone."*
(Psalm 91:11-12)

Which part of this scripture most resonates with you?

_____

_____

_____

_____

_____

_____

_____

Where in your life do you need these words?

_____

_____

_____

_____

_____

_____

_____

How would your life change if you applied this lesson?

_____

_____

_____

_____

_____

_____

_____

Name three things for which you are grateful today:

1)_____

_____

2)_____

_____

3)_____

_____

The Serenity Prayer:
God, grant me the serenity to accept the things I cannot change,
the courage to change the things I can, and the wisdom to know the
difference.

Day 35

Opening Prayer: "Be still and know that the power of God is near."

Daily Scripture: *". . . Do not fear, for I have redeemed you; I have called you by name; you are mine. When you pass through the waters, I will be with you, and through the rivers, they shall not overwhelm you; when you walk through fire, you shall not be burned, and the flame shall not consume you." (Isaiah 43:1-2)*

Which part of this scripture most resonates with you?

_____

_____

_____

_____

_____

_____

_____

Where in your life do you need these words?

_____

_____

_____

_____

_____

_____

_____

How would your life change if you applied this lesson?

_____

_____

_____

_____

_____

_____

_____

Name three things for which you are grateful today:

1)_____

_____

2)_____

_____

3)_____

_____

The Serenity Prayer:
God, grant me the serenity to accept the things I cannot change,
the courage to change the things I can, and the wisdom to know the
difference.

Day 36

Opening Prayer: "Be still and know that the power of God is near."

Daily Scripture: *"Behold, I send an angel before you to guard you on the way and to bring you to the place that I have prepared."* *(Exodus 23:20)*

Which part of this scripture most resonates with you?

_____

_____

_____

_____

_____

_____

Where in your life do you need these words?

_____

_____

_____

_____

_____

_____

How would your life change if you applied this lesson?

_____

_____

_____

_____

_____

_____

_____

Name three things for which you are grateful today:

1)_____

_____

2)_____

_____

3)_____

_____

The Serenity Prayer:
God, grant me the serenity to accept the things I cannot change,
the courage to change the things I can, and the wisdom to know the
difference.

Day 37

Opening Prayer: "Be still and know that the power of God is near."

Daily Scripture: *"But they that wait upon the Lord shall renew their strength; they shall mount up with wings as eagles; they shall run and not be weary, and they shall walk and not faint."* *(Isaiah 40:31)*

Which part of this scripture most resonates with you?

_____

_____

_____

_____

_____

_____

Where in your life do you need these words?

_____

_____

_____

_____

_____

_____

_____

How would your life change if you applied this lesson?

_____

_____

_____

_____

_____

_____

_____

Name three things for which you are grateful today:

1)_____

_____

2)_____

_____

3)_____

_____

The Serenity Prayer:
God, grant me the serenity to accept the things I cannot change,
the courage to change the things I can, and the wisdom to know the
difference.

Day 38

Opening Prayer: "Be still and know that the power of God is near."

Daily Scripture: *"Faith by itself, if it does not have works, is dead. . . . Show me your faith apart from your works, and I will show you my faith by my works." (James 2:17-18)*

Which part of this scripture most resonates with you?

_____

_____

_____

_____

_____

_____

_____

Where in your life do you need these words?

_____

_____

_____

_____

_____

_____

_____

How would your life change if you applied this lesson?

_____

_____

_____

_____

_____

_____

_____

Name three things for which you are grateful today:

1)_____

_____

2)_____

_____

3)_____

_____

The Serenity Prayer:
God, grant me the serenity to accept the things I cannot change,
the courage to change the things I can, and the wisdom to know the
difference.

Day 39

Opening Prayer: "Be still and know that the power of God is near."

Daily Scripture: *"For God did not give us a spirit of timidity, but of power and of love and of calm and well-balanced mind and discipline and self-control."* (*2 Timothy 1:7*)

Which part of this scripture most resonates with you?

_____

_____

_____

_____

_____

_____

Where in your life do you need these words?

_____

_____

_____

_____

_____

_____

How would your life change if you applied this lesson?

_____

_____

_____

_____

_____

_____

_____

Name three things for which you are grateful today:

1)_____

_____

2)_____

_____

3) _____

_____

The Serenity Prayer:
God, grant me the serenity to accept the things I cannot change,
the courage to change the things I can, and the wisdom to know the
difference.

Day 40

Opening Prayer: "Be still and know that the power of God is near."

Daily Scripture: *"I can do all things through him who strengthens me." (Philippians 4:13)*

Which part of this scripture most resonates with you?

_____

_____

_____

_____

_____

_____

_____

Where in your life do you need these words?

_____

_____

_____

_____

_____

_____

_____

How would your life change if you applied this lesson?

_____

_____

_____

_____

_____

_____

_____

Name three things for which you are grateful today:

1)_____

_____

2)_____

_____

3)_____

_____

The Serenity Prayer:
God, grant me the serenity to accept the things I cannot change,
the courage to change the things I can, and the wisdom to know the
difference.

CONGRATULATIONS! YOU DID IT!

Now, let's incorporate what you've learned:

Step 1-Set aside some time to review your answers for the past forty days. What patterns do you see? What surprised you? Which scriptures were the hardest for you to engage? Why? Which were the easiest? What do you think are your most important lessons?

Use the space below to jot down your thoughts. (Remember, there's extra space at the end!)

Step 2-Take a day to sit with your answers from Step 1. Think about the lessons. Pray about them.

Step 3-When you are ready, make a covenant with yourself based on what you've learned. Fill out the form on the next page. Take a photo of it and keep it on your phone. Or cut out the page and put it on your refrigerator, or put it by your bedside table.

Whatever you do, keep it close to remind you of this beautiful gift you gave yourself!

To complete our journey, let's add an extra special touch! At the end of our prayers, we usually say, "Amen." A translation from the Hebrew for "amen" is "so be it." I love adding that phrase. It brings an extra sense of determination and commitment to our words of prayer.

So, let us end our journal with:

AMEN.
So be it.

(And remember, while the journal may be done,

it's just the beginning of the journey!)

MY COVENANT

I _____ commit to doing the
following five things every day that will bring me more grace-filled
gratitude and joy:

#1 _____

#2 _____

#3 _____

#4 _____

#5 _____

AMEN.
So be it.

STAY IN TOUCH!

I hope you have enjoyed this journal and found some new grace-filled gratitude in your life. Now we've got to keep it going! Here are some ways:

SIGN UP for my FREE bi-weekly newsletter, *The Shiny Side Up*, which shares infectious inspiration that will lift you up, make you smile, and leave you stronger! http://susansparks.com/connect/

READ a few of my books. Try my award-winning first book, *Laugh Your Way to Grace: Reclaiming the Spiritual Power of Humor*. Featured by *O, The Oprah Magazine*, this book shares a humorous, yet substantive look at the power of humor in transforming our life, work, and spiritual path.

My second book, *Preaching Punchlines: The Ten Commandments of Comedy*, shares how the tools of standup comedy can transform preaching—and all forms of communication.

How about generating some Christmas cheer any time of the year? Try my best-selling and multi-award-winning book, *Miracle on 31st Street: Christmas Cheer Any Time of the Year—Grinch to Gratitude in 26 Days*!

And keep an eye out for my newest book, *Love, a Tiara, and a Cupcake: Three Secrets to Finding Happy,* which will be available for purchase on Amazon beginning in February 2021.

WATCH and LISTEN to my weekly sermon broadcast every Sunday at 11AM EST from the historic Madison Avenue Baptist Church in New York City, or subscribe to our sermon podcast and listen later at your convenience. http://mabcnyc.org/worship/live-streaming/

INVITE me to guest preach or speak (live or virtual) in your community! I'd love to share some joy!

LIKE/FOLLOW my Facebook and Instagram pages (links on SusanSparks.com), where you'll find more joy and gratitude ideas.

SHARE. If this journal has brought joy into your life, share it with others. Show them some love! Send them a note, tell them how much they mean to you, and include the journal as a gift.

For more ways to keep in touch, check out my website: SusanSparks. com.

I look forward to hearing from you!

AUTHOR BIO

As a trial lawyer turned standup comedian and Baptist minister, Susan Sparks is America's only female comedian with a pulpit. A North Carolina native, Susan received her B.A. at the University of North Carolina, her law degree from Wake Forest University, and her Master of Divinity at Union Theological Seminary in New York City.

Susan has been the senior pastor of the historic Madison Avenue Baptist Church in New York City for twenty years (and is the first woman pastor in its 170-year history). Her work with humor, healing, and spirituality has been featured in *The New York Times* and *O, The Oprah Magazine,* and has appeared on such networks as ABC, CNN, CBS, and the History Channel.

A featured TEDx speaker and a professional comedian, Susan tours nationally with a stand-up Rabbi and a Muslim comic in the Laugh in Peace Tour. In addition to speaking and preaching, Susan is the author of four books and writes a nationally syndicated column through Gannett that is distributed to over six hundred newspapers, reaching over twenty-one million people in thirty-six states.

Most importantly, Susan and her husband, Toby, love to fly-fish, ride their Harleys, eat good BBQ, and root for North Carolina Tarheel basketball and the Green Bay Packers.

Find out more about Susan at SusanSparks.com!

<u>EXTRA PAGES TO REFLECT</u>

<u>BLANK PAGES TO DOODLE, NOODLE, AND THINK</u>

Made in the USA
Middletown, DE
04 January 2021

30745386R00064